THE UNKNOWN CIVILIAN
ANTONY OWEN

KFS

Newton-le-Willows

Published in the United Kingdom in 2020
by The Knives Forks And Spoons Press,
51 Pipit Avenue,
Newton-le-Willows,
Merseyside,
WA12 9RG.

ISBN 978-1-912211-49-4

Supported using public funding by
ARTS COUNCIL
ENGLAND
LOTTERY FUNDED

THE UNKNOWN CIVILIAN

Contents

Part I – The End & the Beginning

A Black Nurse Tends to Wounds   11
The Last Minute of Wilfred Owen's Life   12
John's Wardrobe   13
The Projectionist's Lullaby   14
Arboretum, 1919   15
The Munitionettes FC   16
Toll   17
Two Senryu   18
A Filicide of Flags   19
Animals and Monsters in Men   20

Part II – Journey to World War II

Senryu for Guernica   23
A Week Before the Nanking Massacre   24
Doodlebug   25
A Polish Pilot Dances Over the Sea   26
Sikh Soldier   27
Lidice   28
A German Soldier in Russian Boots   29
The Shiny Woman   30
Stalingrad   31
Song for a Yellow Star Belt   32
P.O.W.   33
Pearl   34
Enola Gay   35
Love Letter from a Kamikaze Pilot   36
Last Kiss for Hiroshima   37
Rape Seed   39
Madonna of Nagasaki   40
Where Widows Wash in Hiroshima   41

An Angered Poet Demands I Write a Poem for Nanking   42

ANONanking#1   43

ANONanking#2   44

The Joy   45

India   46

A Korean Soldier is Blown in Half   47

Part III – The Invisible

The Suicide of Private John Doe   51

For Syrian Boys Who Will Never Kiss a Woman   52

Valentine's Day for Invisible People   53

The Surprise Welcome Home Party   54

The Shrine of Soldier X   55

The Homeless Paratrooper   56

How to Find the Falkland Islands   57

Rwanda   58

Jesus to a Wavering Atheist   59

Part IV – Displaced

To Build a Syrian House   63

The Unfashionable Death of Another Syrian Daughter   64

The Bombing of Beautiful Birds   65

When it Snows in Aleppo   66

Astronauts   67

Rohingya and Other Invisible Places   68

Yemen Tower   69

Hiroshima Brides   70

These Are Not British Waters   71

Part V – Nuclear Families

Dead Babes Stolen for Nuclear Tests   75

Guam   76

Letters of Last Resort   77

Maralinga   78

One Nagasaki Samurai   79

Part VI – Stolen Things

Hamas	83
The Mathematics of Peace	84
Rambo of Kinshasa	85
The Palestinian Song Contest	86
Final Solutions	87
Jerusalem	88
The Star of Gaza	89
Go Home He Said	90
What Churchill Said by the Feet of Jesus Christ and Gary Oldman	91
Belfast on Weather Reports	92
43rd Birthday	93
The Gonorrhea Soldiers	94

Part VII - Nine Eleven & the Hidden Massacres

The Falling Man	97
Flight 93	98
Baghdad Zoo	99
The Bear of Sarajevo Zoo	100
Three Landay Poems for an Afghan Sunrise	101
To Pull the Head From a Flower	102
Srebrenica Massacre	103
War Bird	104
A Woman Soldier Opens Fire	105
Instructions on a Successful Remembrance	106
Imagining Wilfred Owen's 104th Birthday	107
A Syrian Slam Poet Dies with Her Mouth Open	108
Notes	109
Acknowledgements	114

Part I:
The End & the Beginning

"It is a great life. I am more oblivious than alas! yourself,
dear Mother, of the ghastly glimmering of the guns
outside and the hollow crashing of the shells.

There is no danger down here – or if any, it will be well
over before you read these lines"

– Extract from the last letter Wilfred Owen
   sent to his Mother just days before the Armistice.

A Black Nurse Tends to Wounds

By morning the dead turn bottle-green,
pouring their vapours back to the reborn sun.
We do not tell the dying that the Lord never sent his sign.
I shall tell you of the crow and mockingbird that war made unnatural.

Last night I heard a mockingbird mimic the cries across the plateau.
I heard a nickering horse and the sound a tree makes when it dies.
Today I was watching a crow steal lint and viscera from a man,
last week he placed a name in my ear, so heavy it felt.

By dusk I rub gin beneath my nostrils and pray,
there once was a hymn my mother sang that healed me.
In Dominica it was the west wind cleaned by the tears of Jesus
she told me as a child that if I hurt I should let the Lord in to heal me.

Last week the colours ran from war, Ceylon to Coventry, black to white.
With bloodstained khaki we turned the horse troughs purple.
The bandy-legged nags took their bodies to a lime trench,
all of their bones shall be white and grow as red opiates.

I should mention that I am a black nurse in white man's world of war.
My hardest battle is tending to a wound that keeps reappearing,
there was a boy that would not leave my eyes as he went,
"You're an Angel" he said. My wings were black, broken.

The Last Minute of Wilfred Owen's Life

(i) Crossing the canal

A soldier cannot withstand his heart's artillery.
Like a drummer boy's, it knows the ebb and flow of fear.
Did you know that a typewriter was pounding your laid bare soul?

This is the last minute of Wilfred Owen's life under fire and water.
A half-written poem the world never knew bled with him,
the machine gunner's anthem smashed their full stops.

(ii) Cheerio then

It is vital to be polite and wish your chums cheerio, dying gentlemanly.
A poet who writes from his wounds uses the blackest ink.
It curlicues into water as he floats like a sonnet read by a tipsy Irishman.

(iii) The dead orchestra

There is no armistice for soldiers who know the fib of poppies,
who know that the dead blow black bugles of fungi.
They go on for miles where the iron soil disturbs.

(iv) Glorious

Let's do this properly and write war poems with etiquette,
the glorious soldier, mouth permanently unlocked.
Write something in Latin to dress death elegantly.

(v) The woman poet

Come, pawn me the mad metal cross in jewellers across Wirral,
come wear me a poem, brand my ears with Dulce Decorum.
Last night a nurse read her war poem to tin soldiers of shell-shock.

John's Wardrobe

They grew herbs on the Badlands,
thyme and coriander brought the tilling worms
but the farmhouse was still a slave-ship you could smell a mile away.

There was not a single man a mile away, all of them were dead or mad.
Pears rotted in the wind of a twenty-thousand final-breaths,
a war maddened mother stabbed herself in the ovaries.

There are no sons here but fragrance,
a tree sprawls through a tractor engine like hands of a mother in his clothes.
John's wardrobe is open today, she is letting him go and he floods the house.

John's sheepdog lost the will to herd
she scratched four lines into his bedroom door
raking her grief, she is the sentry of his room and finds him there.

If the sun was a brass button of the fallen it would come loose in the sky,
it would glimmer on grey skin like sky itself was a corpse,
the glory of God is a white tunic covering the dead.

The Projectionist's Lullaby
After Garrie Fletcher

I leave only in my mirror moon,
our prosthetic copper mask unclasps
revealing the glories that make you cry.

I find solace in French girls in hour rooms
who blow out rings of Woodbine to moths
and apply masks to conceal the city gents' fists.

My sanctuary is above the Draylon trenches,
where cigar smoke hangs, like poor Clive,
from ropes of light that bring the beautiful

Dietrich in mink purring the lover's line
Edna Yates spooled into my lobe
the night before she out wept trains on Lime Street.

I sweep up the kisses left on tissues.
My half face sinking in the lighthouse
while the war awaits me on Civvy Street.

I project a Hollywood lion to roaring Scousers,
fasten faces that burnout at the end
and then I'm a film star, Passchendaele's Frankenstein.

Arboretum, 1919

Stonemasons blew a sandstone fog,
wren and chisel did their slow work
in nests that never finish.

Long ago, when peace broke out
a ring of prams circled the crib.
God is looking for the missing names:
O'Brien,
         Kaur
                 Mackie
                         Anglicised Colonials.

The babies cried out for their mothers *like soldiers,*
the mothers cried out for their lovers like humans.
A bugle missed a key note for death in discordance.

The Munitionettes FC
For Katy Wareham Morris

One day a week smoke cleared over Merseyside to become a stadium roof.
After each match women bathed and passed carbolic soap like communion bread.
Their bodies were no man's land. Their wrinkles filled with mud entrenched with lovers gone.

Fifty thousand women watched every game bar a few men without faces or legs.
Some women hung over railings like dirty linen as laughing peelers made jokes.
Have you ever seen the beautiful game played like a war without mercy by women?

In factories they sieved cordite into metal like flour onto pastry.
One woman was punched unconscious for stealing rags for her period,
they later found out she was five months gone and miscarried.

In factories were motes of teal rain disturbed by pigeons nesting in asbestos.
Below them were women with skin yellowed by trinitrotoluene –
they called them canaries, and on match day how they sang.

One Friday in the factory the striker wore clogs to prevent sparks near cordite.
On Saturdays she set the grass on fire with a goal from thirty yards,
she gave her lips to a man without a face to make him feel alive.

To this day those allotments you see were most likely dug by women.
In Passchendaele they pull marrows out of the ground with bones wrapped in root.
In Wembley the English women's football team are behind, but they have already won.

Toll

These valeted suits the stiff men starched
face floating names with whom they marched
that roll from stone the sunlight parched.

These tasselled flags roll with throats
a bagpipe snags against its notes
carolled rags have sailed like boats.

The empty chairs shall fill with rain,
hollowed youth will leave their stain
signing up to belong again.

Stems from England's bloodied rose –
a vase of sky with kerosene bows
the blooming buds that had to close.

War speaks through tongues of maddened bells
and locked in men with mouths like wells
that hang like mist in check out hotels.

The men and women who all come back
lions and lambs confined to a pack
who stroke their friends on the acre plaque.

And so, it is the war we've built
old over young in six foot of silt
our ceremonies of grandeur guilt.

Two Senryu

"The English may batter us to pieces, but they will never succeed in breaking our spirit."

– Maud Gonne

Senryu for The Irish Massacre

Save Ireland there, *here*,
bang mud from dead brother's boots
O'er his unmarked grave.

Senryu for a boy shot for cowardice

Freckle me in steel
one bullet for each year lived,
scarlet ribbons gush.

A Filicide of Flags

For glories then, this filicide of flags
the sweet meadows cul-de-sacs
fellows marching home on skittish nags.
Those bulbous sacks their stories then
told to children in sodden sheets
faces empty as Kitchener's streets.

For glories then, the numbered hymns
a quaint parish amongst the slums
victorious then those slumbered limbs
paint garish medals of jingoistic drums
and Ha'penny flowers the war office sent
died on the typeface all withered and bent.

Animals and Monsters in Men

Those Belgian butchers are buying all the crazed horses –
haggling on the price, saying they're full of shrapnel.
War makes blacksmiths out of butchers and butchers out of blacksmiths.

Trenches are troughs now, where foxes drink from,
and tell-tale crows, plump messengers of war,
harrow their beaks through nationless flesh.

The tavern-talk of god-fearing men down our village
afraid to tell to the vicar's wife she's right about everything,
that people come back in the flesh but not so in the eyes.

I've seen monsters in men tending to the bald horses,
they are trying to break them, they are all broken.

Part II:
Journey to World War II

A German officer visited Picasso in his Paris studio during the Second World War. There he saw the painting of Guernica and, shocked at the modernist chaos of the painting, asked Picasso: "Did you do this?" Picasso calmly replied:

"No, you did this!"

– Slavoj Žižek

Senryu for Guernica

You were the chosen,
Picasso mixed his paints red,
primary colours.

A Week Before the Nanking Massacre

"When gods sleep the monsters in men wage war"

– Anon

Unregistered baby born on an eyeless night
the gods never saw your beginnings so let us go back.
Nine months ago, you were made by a murdered river,
back then the waters ran pure and you were the light.
Nine months ago, you were made with love in a storm
sky was so heavy that it carried the heat of your makers.
Your makers were a seamstress and a leather cutter.
When they cut you from her the sun bled over water,
let us not talk of the events that come in eight days.

Let us talk of the event that came eight days later.
Six Japanese soldiers held you into the decaying moon,
splayed threads they made from your body, made god weep,
sun threw its bayonets all over the world in fury.
Let us talk of the thousands like you and say *it happened,*
that Nanking and Hiroshima are unconnected atrocities.
A woman said. *"We should not quote numbers but names"*
If I said sorry for the avoiders would it make us see you?
You, *my* child, *my* beautiful human daughter of the gods.
I see you
grieve you
give you
life.

Doodlebug
(Senryu)

Random murderer,
we hear you humming through clouds
sad Aryan songs.

A Polish Pilot Dances Over the Sea
For Alec Newman

I understand why you never bailed out
to watch those entrails of smoke as merlin groaned,
the spidery glass from the bullet which made your skin North Sea grey,
I understand why you kissed St Christopher as you shot Poseidon, *your last voyage.*

Last sortie you saw silky graves of men who bailed out over sea to die thirsty.
You would never go out this way in the mournful psalter of waves
for tide to leave your parachute like a tentacled jellyfish
for boys to unwrap your body as a crab left your eye.

I understand why you never made love to Sylvia,
to lay her down in wheat and plough her eyes for meaning.
You should know that she watched you fall like her tresses that night
when you sank into her mouth and floated above brass and a poor man's Vera Lynn.

Men like you are the lint we see from vast blue sheets we washed and hung out to dry,
we pick that lint and wind picks it up to take it back to the endless sky.
Men like you dance like Sylvia and Messerschmitt kite tails,
this is the last waltz, and the band leaves to silence.

Sikh Soldier

'Britain did not fight the second world war, the British Empire did.'

—Yasmin Khan

We had a chance to unravel their turbans in winter breaths.
Your stories are hidden in the stoic geriatric.
He is locked in eyes dementia blue.
It is too late now erstwhile friend.
Chime the bedpan it is time.
Float like stalled spitfires.
It is too late now and
breathe blue turbans
watch them unravel.
It is too late now.
Had our chance.
Singh, Lion,
brave hero.
Fearful of
the foe.
Death
go
.

We had a chance to write a poem shaped in saluting chevrons.
Your great grandson unearthed you in itchy khaki.
He is locked in your life, eyes wide and blue.
It is never too late when eyes burn tatters.
They are immaculate in memoriam.
Men never look happy as soldiers:
they strut into instructed death.
The truth is not unexpected,
a mosquito killed him.
Hokkaido nights are
darker than urine.
No water here,
no humanity,
no England.
Just land.
Just war.
Just man.
Unjust.

Lidice

With each sped up massacre
birds shot out from trees with each shaking luger.
Let me report the apple orchard of drunk soldiers and wasps.
Let me edit out the keen underling inebriated on cleansing a whole town.

With each slowed down massacre
I see men in rows of ten queue to meet their unmaker.
I see children humanised then germanised then heavenized.
Let me edit out the beautiful daughter now, gargoyle of the cruel miasma.

With each decade Lidice moves a yard further from the surface.
Take my hand and walk us in single file to the orchard trees.
Tell me that fascist butchers are ashamed of their meat,
how they rush bury the remains and how guilt eats them.

Tell me that the ride to Lodz for the children was short.
That they never slept in their urine on *Gestapo* floors.
Tell me that their faces never went haggard in fog.
Show me that all the things I know are too evil.

A German Soldier in Russian Boots
After Max Hastings & Willy Reese

Comrade, your thigh meat tasted like game and leather.
I needed your boots, so hung you over a fire to loosen them.
Your winters are so cold that my piss comes out like red fire.

Comrade, your eyes have thawed and it looks like you're crying.
Wolves are lapping the chummed snow and I feel nothing.
I am tame to them; their numbers expand like gun-metal.

Comrade, did you know old German newspapers blow all over Russia?
They come from trench-coats of Fuhrer's phantoms.
Your winter shall win you this war come summer.

It's so cold that I shot the oil from a panzer and made myself a skin.
My crimes are safe behind my perfect sky-blue eyes.
Aryan boys die like dogs, live white as statues.

Comrade, I defiled your body because I needed your boots.
I hacked into the ice with my blade like you were meat,
and you were meat, you were my footsteps home.

It's so typical that I am to die beneath the Soviet sickle moon.
My cause of death – a toe that slowly gnawed my left leg.
Comrade, the motherland is full of brothers in arms.

The Shiny Woman

In the train carriage we left our pelts of men, and
war made our demon from boot polish on virgin skin.
Steal a woman once and repeat over through liquor.
We made her dance, made her intoxicated in collective madness.

Endless snow and the petrified dead can make a man impure.
So, the beast and eagle hurl crowns into eyes of men;
makes them devils, makes them slaves that make slaves.
We smeared boot polish on her breasts to turn her black as us.

We made her drunk as we were.
We made her mad as we were.
We made her.
She unmade us.

Stalingrad

In Stalingrad a flag sways with peasants,
the gibbets are wind chimes.
Children are eating the starved,
with eyes drunk on darkness.

The earth is too hard for crops,
sickles no longer draw breath,
Tanks no longer swerve to avoid bodies,
snow-flakes only melt on the living.

Vodka made the Germans sing aloud.
One of them wept, sipping from a rifle.
A Mother poured barley on a soldier's wound
she said "Death's the only enemy here."

They all took turns inside her,
one of them flicked Deutschmarks;
"This will buy us bread" she said.

Song for a Yellow Star Belt

In the square
they are beating men to classical music.
Last year they danced in this spot, the same children watched.

In the square
a local orchestra kneels before its composer.
He is made to throttle the defiant celloist with piano strings.

All things pass,
ignore the old shoemaker covering the breasts of his dead wife:
in five years, he will watch from the patisserie as kids chalk hopscotch.

All things pass,
like the twitching general damned by the sleight seamstress.
He thought she closed her eyes, but she snared him in a blink shot.

In the orchestra,
a solitary flutist set free an excerpt of the murdered crescendo.
I swear a whole crowd gathered in the square to hear it soar like black fireworks.

P.O.W.

"To forgive is to set a prisoner free and discover the prisoner was you"
– Lewis B. Smedes

In a chime choke Alms house
his eyes bled out Hokkaido
like blackberries in Tupperware.

He weaved baskets in whimpering huts,
for guards who wickered his skin
painted in skeins of osier.

A skeleton gave him maggots
to feast on lacerated smirks.
When they were fat he ate them.

His wife was the prisoner of war
refusing to be liberated,
dying with his ear lobe litany.

That night he escaped to Brighton
by unfolding the myrrh of her wrists,
which later she pared like a herring.

Pearl

"I fear all we have done is to awaken a sleeping giant and fill him with a terrible resolve"

— Admiral Isoruku Yamamoto, 'Tora, Tora, Tora' (1970)

You woke the sleeping giant by his vast ocean,
soon he will emerge from the stars as you did the sun.
Yours will be hundreds of *Zeke* suns on wings of dragons.
Yours will be two fiery eggs where the phoenix will eat Hiroshima, Nagasaki.
In war there are sons and daughters branded by flags hoisted to spirits.
I picture the moaning ships rising up, gulping American blood.
I picture the teeth of split hulls swallowing immigrant sons,
these steel vampires will carry night and nuclear sun.

Is this darkness blacker than atomic shadows?
They are not to be connected, just grieved for.
American, Irish, American Irish or Sioux Indian.
This was your day of infamy returned twice-fold.

Enola Gay

It all makes sense now, for sky is a storyteller.
Enola in the mirror reads as "Alone," *so let us reflect then.*
Let us be gay for a moment and think of a survivor dying peacefully.

Picture this:
thousands saw Enola Gay
like a silver crucifix left on a crushed blue velvet sky.

Capture this:
bamboo spears, some unsharpened,
children used them to stir clothes in carbolic water.
They pierced only sky and smoke made flutes of them.

Oh, Enola Gay,
you were a mother who made children and boysenberry pie
one summer day.
You were *the other* who took children and lifted them to sky.

Oh, Enola Gay,
your son wrote your name as doomsday on a silver crested bird.
You danced as a naked flame and candled flesh till cicadas chirred.

It all makes sense now, for black rain was war bathing in its madness.
When I think of Enola Gay, she was a mother with a crucifix,
it faced the right way up; her blood was dragon warm.

Oh, Enola Gay,
another Hibakusha has died today,
she was a little girl who used to wait for her Mama and say:
"The soul of my bloodline is in the sky, so each night I shall pray"

Love Letter from a Kamikaze Pilot
June 1945, Kure, Japan

Down here Sumiko,
stars twitch like silkworms
and I am just a reel spun from sky
on half spun whorls of smoke and rising sun in free-fall.

Down here Sumiko, I saw an emperor moth fall like me.
Some flames pulse like your chest against mine.
I have dishonoured the wind with my blade.
Cut down men like pale sighing corn.

Up there Sumiko,
I sail blue sky to surface ship or sea.
The ink of this letter dried where Sika deer drink;
they do so cautiously, looking in every direction for prey.

Honour me Sumiko,
go to Hiroshima as it blossoms and
when they scatter white frocks. I have married you.
Start a new life there, but take my Mother pink chrysanthemums.

Last Kiss for Hiroshima

(i) Woman standing on the ruins

Staring into space counting dying stars and Japanese suns
a mandible of teeth smiles through a soffit –
oh woman, standing on the ruins, what did you see in the sky?

(ii) Raggy Girls

They called them the raggy girls, all in terrible kimonos,
skin blowing from their fingernails like silk on the line.
Blood is blue in gamma rays, like Hiroshima rivers.

(iii) Trinity

After Trinity they found nuclear emeralds of sand turned to glass
seeing an opportunity, they soldered these into lockets
for patriots to wear beautiful cancer timebombs.

(iv) A man photographs the Hypocentre

Two weeks afterwards and breaths still rose from the hypocentre.
You photographed a man melted into the arms of his baby.
In the red room their faces emerged through water.
Thank God for such small mercies.

(v) Three hours after the explosion on Miyuki Bridge

Two kilometres from the devil's heart souls fill the wet ventricles.
A policeman soaks mercurochrome onto silent rocking children.
The cradles rock in kaleidoscopic heat waves that taste metallic.

(vi) Statues

I have never seen a statue shoot up from stone like a root.
If you look close enough into her contortions you see
pink valleys where the devil-wind never reached.

(vii) An educated man tells me the atomic bomb was justified

Young child, your words are somewhere to be found by yourself.
You are branded Japanese, so deserve to die for what you did.
Young babies cry without their mothers, so we will take them too.

(viii) An educated man tells me the atomic bomb was still justified

See: VII, VI, V, IV, III, II, I.

Rape Seed

The bald crow was not itself.
Its mange maddened caw hushed cicadas.
The fingering wings afraid to touch the blue betraying sky.

The pipistrelles ignited where they bivouacked.
At night their hearts glow like dim lanterns.
They are emitting the souls of Hiroshima.

The dead reek of fish hung like Alaskan salmon.
Zombies return to where their homes once stood.
How could they know this? Nothing is here.

These zombies have a second sense where home is,
like that scene in Romero's Dawn of the Dead
they gather at the mall to be consumed by what consumed them.

The flowerheads are blotchy with bees
soused from strange pollen. They are the pulse of heaven.
Lucifer is admiring the wet black seeds of man turned god.

The hives all wept colonies and royal jelly.
A Sika deer laps the golden palaces and falls over a cliff.
There are so many of god's animals smashed against the rocks.

Lucifer watches the rape of Mother Nature.
Man is unborn.

Madonna of Nagasaki

Of all the bodies startled in mid-stride or flounder
there was one of a woman balled over a shape with milk teeth.
It is three days after the sky was scalped by man and now pilgrims make Salem.

In the mile-long Mitsubishi plant Korean songs stay lost upon the rooftops.
Many smoked Virginian leaves up there, blowing halos into sky
twice stolen. They were the closest to God at eleven zero two.

The Madonna of Nagasaki was decapitated and stared at all who grieved or gloated.
Her eyes of crystal streamed down the scorched side of her cheek, and
someone left a radioactive prayer book close to her mouth.

This is a prayerless place, where no one is Japanese and (in)human.
Shapes converge at stone and wail at an heirloom of mandible.
A baby suckles a tit and dies a million times in the eyes of man and

Madonna just stares, *Sensei Nagasaki.*

Where Widows Wash in Hiroshima
After Professor R Klein

To baptise her first-born she only used water untouched by bodies.
Fat from monsters the eels split their skins and gulls came for miles.
Sky became a war-ground of corvid families,
a bomb can alter nature itself.

To feed her first-born she took him to the wet nurse in Kure.
Mothers of 'fire kissed by dragons' would wash in the sea,
teasing out pus with lavender oil, hoping for milk.
One of them swam out to an Icarus sun.
She washed up in moonlight and milk.

I have heard a voice break like Nagasaki shells,
where pram wheels squeaked like frightened mice,
and dead bodies moved from lice ridden cloth.
Dignity can kill if you value all that was not to be,
like widows washing keloids in nuclear darkness.

I have heard of a blinding light turning hands to white flowers.
how in utero her baby wrote its hand across her skin,
she swore it would arrive still as sick grey suns.
I have seen the tweezers she used to mine glass.
"Fifty-three pieces I removed," she insisted.

An Angered Poet Demands
I Write a Poem for Nanking

An angered poet held my book The Nagasaki Elder and demanded to know:
"why have you not written about Nanking and the hushed rapes?"
He told me the Japs got what they deserved, and we argued.

I said that I know of Hiroshima and her lesser known sister.
An elder from Nagasaki was six years old when she trod into ghosts.
The first was an intermingled ribcage of horse and thighbone of man, a centaur.

I asked him if this girl got what she deserved and he told me I should be ashamed.
Last week I watched a film called Dunkirk and it was about Dunkirk.
They missed out the earlier crimes of British soldiers in Ireland because the film was about Dunkirk.

I wrote two poems for Nanking and one was about Nanking.
The other poem was about mixing war crimes, and the only rhymes that matter
are poems for the nationless flesh connected by stanzas ending abruptly like this.

ANONanking#1

In the neon atrocities
we kissed in static rain
a monsoon glued us with water.

Is Nanking more than a war crime?
I should write something, yes,
let us revisit the crime scene.

There is an empire of ectoplasm,
you could a lay a railroad of bone
and close your eyes on the ghost train.

A prisoner of war is someone who denies it –
the bayoneted baby born of liquored rage,
a flag stabbing God in the bloody eye.

A poet who wrote clever poems about nothing
told me I must write of the Nanking massacre,
he destroyed Hiroshima as I helped rebuild it.

I want to watch wheels of Nanking rainwater splash in the puddles,
keep you separate to Hiroshima, not contaminate the crime scenes.

ANONanking#2

Unregistered baby born on an eyeless night,
the gods never saw your beginnings so let us go back.
Nine months ago, you were made by a murdered river,
back then the waters ran pure and you were the light.
Nine months ago, you were made with love in a storm
sky so heavy that it carried the heat of your makers.
Your makers were a seamstress and a leather cutter.
When they cut you from her the sun bled over water,
let us not talk of the events that come in eight days.

Let us talk of the event that came eight days later.
Six Japanese soldiers held you into the decaying moon,
splayed threads they made from your body, made god weep,
sun threw its bayonets all over the world in fury.
Let us talk of the thousands like you and say it happened,
that Nanking and Hiroshima are unconnected atrocities.
A woman said. "We should not quote numbers but names."
If I said sorry for the avoiders would it make us see you?
You, my child, my beautiful human daughter of the gods.
I see you,
grieve you,
give you
life.

The Joy

Since nineteen twelve that tree recorded the sky –
a marriage of wood and stars. Until the glitch.
The fiery sore that cleaved you open.
An etched heart, arrow and
names in penknife kanji.

They circle the Aogiri tree,
like Nagasaki streetcars on inertia.
The passengers burnt where they stood.
A passage of static lifting their hair like fans.
Married to atoms they chanted names to *Yeshua*.

A man once told me of the joy.
He saw a black rain of starlings over the sea,
his boat drifted into the nothingness and listed,
that moment he smiled so wide his gums bled burgundy.
The joy he felt lifted like the silver phosphate of his young bride.

The joy
are screams ending
like stretched silk rending.

The joy
are orphans gekkering
like hearts full of lettering.

The joy
are Hibakusha giving,
all the lost lives to all of the living.

India

Carve India like ivory,
wash the shade of your bloodstained hands to Atlas-pink.
Tomorrow, you will shatter ancient land anew with genteel white hands.

A Korean Soldier is Blown in Half
After "Massacre in Korea" by Pablo Picasso, 1951

Think of her not as the enemy,
lowering like a pail to her legs.
Think of her body as north and south.
The mind and eyes its northernmost point,
watching the south part of her drift like continents.

Had I have been born more southerly ninety years ago,
somewhere near a prohibited sea by the bony shale,
would a stork hand me a white feather shrieking?
Would it know of what awaits in the widow-lands?
I think I may be someone different, we'll never know.

A Korean soldier is blown in half. Walk past her.
Go to the DMZ and draw the line in boiling tar.
Use the same brush for friends and constant enemies.
Laugh at how crazy they seem with their daft ways.
Hate them for eating dogs and don't let sleeping dogs lie.

Part III:
The Invisible
PTSD
Battle Fatigue
Shell Shock
Madness

"Get together like brothers, but work together like strangers."

– Iraqi Proverb

The Suicide of Private John Doe

I wonder in those brief PayPal unions
of credit card wanks and smileys
if hotgirl97 misses you at all.

I wonder if Ray got home after mourning you
those twenty-two days of hard whiskey,
fighting to be heard by headless suits.

I wonder if Bob at Wickes saw the rope
as he scanned it through and thought
that aint pulling no tree down.

I wonder which random thing set you off,
was it Afzal in Texaco holding your tenner to the sun,
or a cherry short on a scratchcard?

Pam in Tesco told Babs at the checkout
that she heard you were found all blue and that
whilst a man hung a lamb for the world to see.

I heard your Ma tell your sister in her belly
that heroes are ghosts of cold sons
born grey on the sleeves of a stonemason.

At least, that's what she means in those silences
when thumbnail faces of soldiers come home
in televisions and rope whilst Pam whispers loudly of loss.

For Syrian Boys Who Will Never Kiss a Woman

When tornadoes come
clouds roll tightly like judicial wigs and
war maddened children stare blankly into space.
Their heads are gavels metering out unseen sentences.

Up there in dreadful totems
climb the flesh and bone of descendants.
An abacus of crows bickers from telegraph poles
communicating remnants of meat that whispered tenderly.

When little people die
their bodies are blue watercolours.
An art of war painted by those without ears,
who sell their masterpieces only to those who bid the highest.

Where little people lived,
meats shone like red lamps on market day
and skinny dogs lapped blood in the cobbles
where Mukesh Junior learnt the music of trading.

In the parliament of slow kissing
I told my wife I love her and all the reasons why.
I told her for Mukesh who might not know a woman's lips,
and I told her for myself because at my most simple I am elegant.

Valentine's Day for Invisible People

(i) Soldier

Sometimes you drift back there
when people pluck up the courage
to ask you what it was like out there.
And you think of job centre smiles
when they mean *out there*: in war zones,
and you think of that party at Kev's gaff,
when people fought over Miley Cyrus and if she'd gone too far.

(ii) Refugee

Sometimes you drift back there
when Facebook Kev posts fuck off home.
And meanwhile you fondle Aldi Pomegranates
knowing they are rotten inside, yet people take them.
Yesterday you covered your whole body, except your eyes,
and everyone in the world seemed blindfolded, except for children.

(iii) Widower

Sometimes she returns to you
when Harry introduces you as Joan's husband.
This is how you always stayed until March eighth,
when Harry found you in May as a cold blue ship sailed.
Donning your medals, you must have returned to Agrigento,
silently thinking: *"fuck you Harry and your beige army of Naysayers."*

(iv) Poet

Some of us never returned to poetry
except the time when all of us were poets,
raising hell, or a child, or a cheap glass of plonk;
and all of this was a life you wrote without words.
I have seen a thousand poets hide in the eyes of people,
extraordinary people who thought they were clichés. Alas, you were not.

The Surprise Welcome Home Party

Everything was thought out:
the suffocated spread that your Mother laid out.
How would she know the white defrosted eyes of salmon would break him?
How would she know that his mind is still there?
Everything was badly thought out.

At the surprise welcome home party of the son and fusilier
do not think a salmon with cucumber fins will save him.
Do not let his sister's cocksure boyfriend call him mate.
Do not exchange conversation with him when he is drunk.
It is unnatural to be yourself around someone who will never be again.

An exhaust backfires and the haunted return to war.
It is natural to be born bloody and they wiped him clean so he was anew.
It is unnatural to die bloody from the hands of another.
The trapped mind is a cage of a trillion locks.
It is unnatural to become a ghost.

At the surprise welcome home party there will be carnage.
Just light a candle and leave the door ajar with noise.
There has to be noise and a song he liked.
There has to be a window that opens.
And preferably, no fireworks.

The Shrine of Soldier X

*"Even when I'm dead, I'll swim through the Earth, like a mermaid of the soil,
just to be next to your bones."*

— Jeffrey McDaniel

In her awkward remembrance
she copied and pasted a link to her son.
He was smiling at a city match, we won that day.

Take me to the shrine that his Ma unlocks yearly
to lay foetal shaped where he dreamt
waiting for the day's remains.

Slip away like a pall of interwoven lions.
Give the triangle of England to her.
This is the fabric of his nature.

Take me to the shrine where his Da will just be.
these anniversaries cannot go on; and yet,
they go on and on and on and on.

Slip away and sleep Mr and Mrs X.
Your shrines will be shared and he will live till Tuesday,
until *the last post* on Facebook is interrupted by a like count.

The Homeless Paratrooper

"In some parts of the country they (ex-military) number 12% of the homeless population"
— BBC

The sleeping bag contains her movements.
Twitching in that chrysalis is a pinned butterfly.
I want you to hold her but she is too delicate for human hands.

Five years ago she paused the woman and began transformation.
What people forget about paratroopers is they fall.
Mach-two fire wheezes like a dying devil.

If her head was a lid and I poured you a taste of Afghanistan
it would taste like lamb and the mortuaries of heaven.
The median age of slaughtered meat is nineteen.

If her heart was a doorway it would be locked, yet slightly ajar,
if you knock it means you are not ready to enter.
If she is not there then she is in uniform.

Nine years ago I met a para who told me her name like it still mattered.
She left a world on my shoulders to carry me to safety.
She gave me eyes so I could defend myself.

One year ago I saw the rectangle of where her chrysalis was moved.
Perhaps she will live for a day and spread her colours in the grey.
Perhaps war will catch another butterfly and hide its remains.

How to Find the Falkland Islands

You carry yourself like peat in Port Stanley air.
The authorial eye writes a hundred facial lines.
These are the new trenches frozen under fire.

Have you ever seen a field of wool and knitted limbs?
It's not how many die but how they die over in the mind.
All my friends say so much, yet they say nothing.

I have something to say, but will keep it locked.
Do you know why winds of war are made of black dots?
It is flies who sing above the reeking fallen, *glory be.*

Ken left no note, I get that he was already gone.
He moved like an Argentinian tango under fire.
A scripted rejection in the Job centre killed him.

We used to laugh at penguins falling over as jets went overhead.
They would look at the unnatural as far as their heads bent back.
It was the weight that took them over, I know that weight well.

Ken told me to fuck off when I tried to dig in him.
Mad as a budgerigar forced to see himself in your cage.
Your fucking cage that made us dress pretty for glory.

You are all blind.
I go eyes wide open
with moon and sun.

Rwanda
After Andrea

A headscarf twitches on the wire.
I am very interested in how it got there,
like shoes of different sizes strewn across a field.
I am very interested in these states of man, *unlike America.*

A Toyota headlamp pops out with wires like a torn-out eye.
I am very interested in webs of smashed in windscreens
and how yellow dust of airbags spray like daffodils
blowing pollen into a human face, eyes open.

I am very interested in these things but do not say "genocide,"
unless it is nine eleven or painted white like Van Gogh lilies.

Jesus to a Wavering Atheist

Last night over Jerusalem
sun motes hung in the air like wood you planed from the methuselah.
I like to think that all the old trees contort with your face from the whip.
I like to think that when your flesh opens blossoms burst out from the bough.

Last night over Coventry,
night came in like ink spilt into dirty grey water, but there was an odd beauty.
In those strands of dark I thought how your hair could not have been blonde,
how you – like the Yemeni child with eyes teeming the dew of old days – were discarded.

Last night over the Trump Wall
a border guard brought in Tacos for his friends and handed them out like disciples,
all of these men go home to boys and girls who yell and whisper "Daddy's home."
I like to think they are good people, like Jesus of Tijuana, wanting a better life for their
kids.

Last night I read a passage from Leviticus, and I am not a religious man,
he beheld the city and wept over it, saying: *"If thou hadst known"*.

Part IV:
Displaced

"Their breaths should have been sufficient as visas"

– The Calais Swaddling

To Build a Syrian House
"Be not water taking the tint of all colours"

– Syrian proverb

Before the cleansing
it was rain that lifted the essence of Syria.
Rape seed was not a covered man hauling God.
The flower-seller yielded lobes of Jasmine not sliced ears and Kalashnikovs.

Before the cleansing
I remember washing your back in the bath,
your toe pressed into the faucet. We were blood in water.
For three nights we lit spirits and tried to make a baby as muezzins wept.

To build a Syrian house you need sage for the bodies we leave in the street.
You need to leave shoes on shallow graves and poison for skinny foxes.
To shut the door of a Syrian house you must say your goodbyes:
say them quietly and always do so in dark wearing dark clothes.

Before the cleansing
we sighed like blades through overgrown grass,
we danced like Russian newspaper pages in God's last street,
and I loved you forever as you went mad saying all is lost, and yet …

I found us.

The Unfashionable Death of Another Syrian Daughter

Knock-kneed from Sarin she walked in perfect ovals.
The girl is being evacuated from her bowels.
Forget that image think of her an hour ago.

Her fingers were jade from ripping coriander for soup.
she combed that smell into her Mothers balding head.
In fifty-eight minutes the whole world will care.

A pilot from Earth once described the explosion of a bomb.
He said it looked like a folded-up Christmas tree.
Down there are people unwrapping their skin.

Back to the girl? Or do we skip forward to the end? *Yes, lets.*
Captain America and Wonder Woman from Tel Aviv came.
They saved them all and the camera zoomed in on the credits.

Daughter of Syria played by a caption of *Coco* by *Chanel.*
Mother of Daughter interrupted by an advert for *Amazon.*
I travelled there last night to order some cologne, *how progressive.*

The end of this poem is random, imagine street dogs sharing meat.
They tear each other to shreds then another dog comes and another.
Leave an emoji at the grave. Share the meat. Shine a bat-light to Aleppo.

Help them.

The Bombing of Beautiful Birds
After Matt Merritt

In the drone slums
a blue niqab fell in the shape of the Euphrates.
Her child became the pallor of an orphan in a split second.
All the children spray out from stone like trapped dandelions,
as if sun itself had decided to struggle out through bomb cracked pavements.

In the marshlands they made a proverb from a reed-warbler they found 'a-wander'.
They taught their children that there are two types of interventions:
the first is American, where they bomb the beautiful birds;
the second is Saleen, who found and nursed the warbler.
Even the egg bandits sliced lemons for grey water.

Long ago in Massachusetts
they loaded grey squirrels in maple cages for grand English mansions.
When oaks wept acorns the greys would devour them all.
In time the reds ran like sudden blood and buzzards picked them off.
This was the thin red line, like blood in Iraqi rivers snaking back to green.

In marshlands of the Euphrates undammed water returned from imprisonment.
A long oarsman stabbed the riverbed as the surge took him by surprise,
balancing like the one-legged bird in silhouette he stayed afloat.
This was how they knew the war was over for a while.
The egg bandit returned to his calling of wood carvings.

When it Snows in Aleppo
After Bejan Matur

It came quickly to take them away.
They never knew if the flames were Russian or British,
but it came nonetheless; and flames can make you so cold if you survive them.

It came slowly in the night for her. And,
I want to say that all the feathers from her exploding pillowcase made Angels
that took her to the place between heaven and the smouldering signposts of hell.

When it snows in Aleppo I hope that a bird made of pillow feathers sings her songs.
I hope that it rests to sip from the scarlet slush and makes a new nest
I hope the snowmen made of people, where they fell, fly away.

When Aleppo thaws I hope we see it.
I hope children stop reaching for red crayons in describing their family
Mothers and Fathers in wax drawings should be circles and sticks smiling on green grass.

Astronauts

I want to stay here in paradise and vote for bream and rice as children shoot each other safely dying like pretend refugees. I want to raise the runt that was tied to the leash of a mongrel and walk it through the ferns and stare south to my homeland and pray. I want to tell my nephew that his Mother and Father were astronauts of water and live floating among the stars that whales blow out to the sky.

Oh, my beautiful friends, I have had to vote for many things that would break your red little ships and sink them in your chests. I have had to vote to leave my daughter, and place my faith in driftwood. I want to stay here in paradise and watch my brother's boy dream and tell him that sea monsters do not yell in Arabic to be saved.

I want to open this locket and tell my wife that the olives here are bitter and how Greek widows stand on towels to collect them for the women. I want to vote for water tomorrow and ask Jurgen why he wears a Leicester top when last year he supported United. I want you to hear how children here pass a football: my turn, your turn, my turn your turn, my turn, my turn my turn, my turn.

They are voting which players they want on their side. They are playing for this camp. They are playing to be children. They are making up the rules.

Rohingya and Other Invisible Places

"How many Rohingya have to die; how many Rohingya women will be raped; how many communities will be razed before you raise your voice in defense of those who have no voice?
        – NOBEL WOMEN'S INITIATIVE,
            open letter to Aung San Suu Kyi from five Nobel Peace laureates

In Rohingya
a bright bird was shunned for being beautiful.
If you see a torc of vultures another village has been burnt down.
Only the river reflects what is happening like stories in another language.

To translate,
a bell is ringing from a dazed Ox circled in fire.
It's only an Ox. He serves the mouth and disputed grass.
At the very same moment in Srebrenica a covered woman unveils her tears.

In Paradise
a man with dirty hands cleans a gold Rolls Royce by day.
At night he scrubs himself and the humming of his wife cleanses him.
England, he says, is gilding Yemen, creating refugees like sadistic Greek Gods.

To translate,
a bell is ringing from a Devon cow, milked for Tesco.
At five a.m. they clean the udders and work them to ulcers.
At the very same moment in Rohingya a landmine clicks, the screen burns out.

To translate,
we are exhausted by death.

Yemen Tower

We could be seen for miles burning,
yet no one saw us except the constant Mir.
Goodnight Britain, our children are hags of sulphur,
we could be heard for miles like heretics of brick and mortar.
No one saw us, except the men who covered their noses, but not their eyes.

If we were in Grenfell would you see us?
Would all the satellites refute the cold grey stars?
Would everything up there have happened yesterday or now?
You could be seen by the Gods freezing as you contemplated our hides.

Hiroshima Brides

She passed like a veiled bride of Hiroshima.
Pale, yet flambéed in a floaty robe that lit the earth,
and clouds covered her beauty so she could go unnoticed.

A blood moon passed us and pulsed like hearts of fallen birds.
A lowly vixen curled around the clearing unnoticed.
"These are the flames that always burnt me," I said.

It's been the longest summer and fake grass glows among the hay.
A couple peel oranges and read long newspapers in bliss.
A blood moon passed them scarred and unnoticed.

My friends, when I am old and a hard rain fills my frown lines,
I want you to tell me I was once beautiful like the Hiroshima brides.
I want you to cover my eyes with sunflowers and smile.

These Are Not British Waters

Sharks care not for international waters.
Dorsal fins slice a sea owned by China,
hardening cocks of plump wealthy men.

Wolves care not for caste of moon.
High on hills their eyes are zodiacs –
a migrant universe wailing to man.

Birds care not for prayers lost in sky.
Palestinian leaves are carried to Israel
and nests of new foundations holler.

Soil cares not for flesh in plywood doors,
or collateral damage skipping in a Spurs top
worn only when mountains weren't looking.

Tarquin cares not for Rashid, prised from a Boeing,
who watched for hours a perfect world from sky.
Before he felt the chill – herds of zebra migrated.

Part V:
Nuclear Families

"It is horrifying that we have to fight our own government to save the environment."

– **Ansel Adams**

Dead Babes Stolen for Nuclear Tests

No one came for your bones, but a gloved hand.
I picture crab-red roads leading to sea as moon peels its violet skin.
No one came for your fossils, so I excavate you.
I picture a mother, who once had dreams empty as a derelict crib.

Skeletons are merely roots growing in ghosts, or their haunted houses.
No one came to ask permission to take your bones.
No one brushed around sand burned to blue glass.
I picture a red birthmark of hell expand into the regurgitated winds.

I am collecting your bones and laying them in a poem.
You would be old now, and yet you will always be young and ancient.
A poet in Oxford is writing a poem about the smell of Wordsworth's cottage.
So, I came for your bones and the weight for one is too much to bear.

I am collecting your bones and I am tired but dare not rest.
Last night I learnt that babies hear songs whilst rowing in uterine.
So yes, I am collecting your bones from the nuclear fires.
I will bury you here in the seed of a poem's full stop.

Guam

Today I wrote my strongest war poem.
I gave it to the easterly wind in the hope it finds Guam.
Each letter swirled into a blank mauve page of tweets I followed.

Yesterday, over Pyongyang, the fingers of a crane wing touched east and west.
In the zig-zag missile stratus it crossed the DMZ and no one noticed.
Each feather was interwoven as the world below came apart.

Tomorrow, in Hokkaido, a siren shoots an artillery of birds into the Sea of Japan
Nobody is sharpening bamboo to protect them from the enemy and friend.
Something enters the airspace and a boy blots a circle into his shorts.

Never told you about the wooden clog a mother found swaying on a splinter.
Days after Hiroshima was bombed a Mother knew it was her daughter's
from a butterfly knot which she tied from her old mauve kimono.

Never told you that Cranes are considered sacred like the red crowned sun:
they house the souls of shadows and fly through sirens that pierce the air like beaks.
A friend told me in Guam there is a different crane that digs a mile-deep silo for peace.

Letters of Last Resort
For Rebecca

I picture him writing the letters of last resort,
scratching a tomb in his best handwriting, in his fine suit.
I picture him as that man from Hiroshima burnt to a shadow.
But, he would be safe in the bowels of Earth painting wine crate buses.

I picture the worst: a submarine commander yelling, "London," yet he is mute.
What if he had a family there and, in that moment, felt a maddening fire.
I picture the atonement on a girl from Moscow, a girl of the womb.
You will be unmade by a man who clips his toenails in bed.

I picture a blue Hiroshima sky, the blueprint of God.
She carried this green seed drenched in her water.
Autumn leaves were her letters of last resort.
I read them once and heard them whisper.

I picture the best, a submarine commander clipping his toenails in bed,
he is watching *The Blue Planet* shaking his head at a dying Polar bear.
The bobbing ice mimics his final breaths starved of food.
That submarine commander weeps, *there is hope yet?*

Maralinga

In tick-tock sand a wing-bone points to Uluru.
Every rock is sacred. A scorpion shapeshifts onto stone.
The Mach-stem took it to heaven and stung God in her eyes.

Men in tee-shirts see white flowers in their hands abloom.
Yes, these are the bulbs of cancer and grow in you like
memories of your children watching you cough red,

white, blue, and all the colours of an England that forgot you.

One Nagasaki Samurai

"The true meaning of the Samurai is one who serves and adheres to the power of love"

– Morihei Ueshiba

For her honour:
steel played out its final note.
She saw pale smoke across the sea,
a fire of his insides, the love, the acts,
one Nagasaki Samurai, his American omen.

For his honour:
she returned as a Mother to Boston,
stroked her swelled belly from left to right
and thought of his sword slicing open his fire *(right to left).*
One American woman, one dragon: kindling to their daughter.

Before the inferno,
was a tiny flame.

Part VI:
Stolen Things

"When you took my land, you stole my Mother
and demanded I give you my name so here it is"

– Anon

Hamas

He who throws a stone should expect boulders

– Anon

Once upon a time, I hid behind my brother.
A bully encroached upon our garden and I threw a punch.
By accident, I hit my brother and we were all covered in his blood.
I hid behind my brother so he could be hit, he trusted me with his life.
Later that night my brothers and I fought, both of us were wailing in secret.

The Mathematics of Peace

Picture an old man with numbers on his arm shuddering by burst gas pipes.
I think he would see the gassing of my child and help me.
I think we could be friends, press each other's wounds.

Picture a sea of children, eyes pitted like Palestinian olives.
Picture them being dragged by the legs to fists.
Six numbers on arms add to nothing.

If I left my house, where would I go, and who would take me?
My children are walking into the sea wanting to die.
This is the sum of forced displacement.

Rambo of Kinshasa

These ghosts were born of water,
surfacing in embryonic filaments.
Your guardian pleased, yet horrified by the acts.

To develop truth you must touch it,
like the soft top of a bloodied firstborn.
Create the life, then hang it from cord.

To speak for the dead we must capture them.
A scabbard of a child pretty last summer.
Her mouth shackled to an elder's flaccid tit.

The laughing taker mining gold from her mouth,
posing on the porch by a half-peeled mandarin,
shouting: "Rambo, you put me as Rambo."

These ghosts are born of water.
Discuss their gifts from the dark place.
Do not speak of their journey here.

The Palestinian Song Contest
For Ann

Inland we were dragged as children from
our homes, aglow like yellow stars.
This is not Orion, but Palestine.

My great grandmother passed down a song.
She passed it down like bread in lace.
Our hearts ripped with that bread.

Welcome to the Palestinian song contest.
My Mother sings to my silent Father.
Equality and borders are wrinkles.

Welcome to the Palestinian song contest.
Israel wins a song for all women. If only
they saw as human first, then woman.

We light a fire where the grass yields to wind.
It is a harsh wind, unrelenting and constant.

Final Solutions

(i) Liberation

When you retched in the raggy soil
was it potatoes growing through a ribcage?
Or a rook's headdress sailing through the cleansed acres?

Liberation is not queuing to leave, some did not want to go,
like the man peeling sky like a loose piece of skin.
He is trying to find the yellow heart of sky.

(ii) Old Children

When you clean that mud from his nails,
tell him it is the very soil his bloodline sails through.
Tell him that a skin sheds a snake with its phial of poison.

(iii) Identity card

You are now reborn, so keep your secrets safe as houses,
but not the homes where humans were reduced to *Juden*.
Your new identity card is a shapeshifter, but will do.

(iv) Gozo

You are now remarried and your wife wore black lace –
a bride for two men, but a heart is just a reflex.
People can love again: warm as Treblinka sleet.

Jerusalem
"Peace cannot be kept by force"

– Martin Luther King

Earth was born a small stone from sling shot stars.
Belonged to all before borders were fault lines.
Goliath was a giant hailed in the yellow sun, star.
I think all the stones have melted like ice in fire.

This is the age of walls being built or knocked down.
I dreamt of cuckoos in Jerusalem threading Acacia from Gaza.
They nested in the safety of mosque, spire, and synagogue. And,
I think the peacemakers with guns never heard that peacefulness.

Oh Jerusalem, a fool sang a ballad and asked wise men to dance to his tune,
and the fool saw a king so vain he was throwing crumbs like stones.
The stones looked big in the disappearing wastelands beyond the wall.
A slum child watches her breath shrink in the window pane and sees Palestine.

Oh, slum child, Gaza is an abaca made up of stones a little boy once held.
You live in skin that is not disputed, yet it craves a place to be childhood.
Oh Jerusalem, your compass pin breaks at west, yet your true north is all.
I am not going to tweet the songs that have come from your millennia.

There is a white house where an ass hee-haws to the birds in Gaza.
Once upon a time lived a family who lived to live and feel alive sometimes.
Nobody would know how a man excavated the shape of his son in linen,
how death wax leaves a fossil of who we were before the claiming.

Oh Jerusalem, the peacemakers with pens and guns will meet in the world.
Land cannot be disputed if we are built of bone and the same blood.
I want to negotiate that I will decide as a citizen of the world
that I will not become a citizen of nowhere. I decide this.

The Star of Gaza
For Ann

The following satellites confirmed Gaza was there –
Sun, moon, unclassified planet Beta-X, and one launched by *Sky*.
Yet, on Earth, no one saw Gaza until it vanished like icebergs in a plastic sea.

Something has malfunctioned in sensors from the Great Wall of Israel.
They are detecting heat signatures of a man hitting cranes with stones.
A soldier has not sensed a human. He shoots the shape to blue.

The following leaders confirmed Hamas was there:
Trump never saw children shot into vegetables whilst tanning on his front,
and Boris never wanted to get into it as Brexit struggled from a Bulldog's ass.

Something has malfunctioned because Gaza is definitely there, *just about*.
A guard of the theft gives a pensioner water then shoots her point blank.
Maybe I never saw that because Gaza is not there in the civilised world.

Go Home He Said

After Tariq Jahan

After all these years of his passing in that slow-mo riot
there is something that sustains through all that you lost.
I once abandoned a magpie twitching at the kerbside.
In my heart I knew it was gone with all its unsung songs.

To bury the dead we must unearth the roots we are from.
"Go home," he said, "Step forward if you want to lose *your* sons."
Blacks whites and Asians when mixed are monochromes.
To develop a picture of the riots add tears and blood of youth.

In ancient Britain, Celts danced around fire to see spirits.
They painted their skins and raked upon coals to find them.
I hope to god that in the ashes of Britain we find Britain.
I hope to god that the ashes of justice do not leave three dead men.

It is cold in the hearth of a street that screeched those endings,
like an urban banshee that keeps wailing *over and over*.
"*Go home,*" he said as he collapsed under the weight of home.
"*Go home,*" he said as he collapsed under the weight of loss.

You once told me of the Syrian woman who cooked you eggs and grass.
"*This is all you have,*" you said, but her son knew your son had left you.
Take those eggs and hatch hope in the nest of the songs he never sung,
like the magpie I could have saved, I can only write you this my friend,

"*this is all I have*".

What Churchill Said by the Feet
of Jesus Christ and Gary Oldman

"This inglorious record of the British suggests that there should be an end to the historical amnesia that prevails in Britain, where a man like Churchill can be deified without any honest reckoning of his record."

– Shashi Tharoor

Oh, plump hero on tallow and polymer,
there are millions of you in circulation.
The five-pound notes are made of fat,
like patient vultures near millions of starved Bengalis –
blood and stomach acid on their right wings.
Oddly always on the right yet paint over it.

"Oh Jesus," Churchill says, *"I am a hero, it was wartime*
I speak the truth of a museum named after me.
I speak the Oscar winning truth of Gary Oldman.
It was wartime and difficult decisions are made,
like two and half million Indian soldiers fighting for Britain,
and three or six million Indians starving for *breeding like rabbits."*

"Oh Winston," Jesus says, *"I poured water into a beggar's mouth*
So murky was this water that I orated a lauded speech for him.
Centuries have taken their vultures and torn quills from them.
They dip them in a liquid darkness editing me white and pure,
my hair not dissimilar to an Aryan yet this was not the true me
Oh, Winston stop cleaning my feet they are bloody enough."

"Oh Jesus," Winston says, *"you are wrong, I am a God,*
to those who worship *The Sun* I am considered a God,
pure as the water you weep for Bengalis, no purer than."

Belfast on Weather Reports

"They have nothing in their whole imperial arsenal that can break the spirit of one Irishman who doesn't want to be broken."

– Bobby Sands

I was eight years old when I first truly saw Ireland.
Michael Fish stuck sunshine over Belfast and it fell off.
They got the weather wrong that week, it rained there.

I was eight years old when I first truly saw England.
Humans smeared a dirty protest over prison walls.
Rib-cages and iron bars served the same purpose.

I was eight years old when I first felt England invade me.
Bobby Sands bled from a mural on a once ordinary house.
Men who never went to Ireland clinked tankards in glee.

I was twenty-one years old when I first felt Ireland.
A horse with a severed rope chewed roses on Dundrum road –
nobody was bothered, *it was bothering nobody.*

I was twenty-one when I first felt England in Dublin.
A stag night from London turned Garda blue and ugly.
It was the end of the troubles, yet cockney lads invaded us.

43rd Birthday

"Suicide is the single biggest killer of men aged under 45 in the UK. In 2015, 75% of all UK suicides were male."

– CalmZone

Unearthing you is a disturbed treasure:
that last glass of red grainy as a *Truprint* sunset;
an immaculate house; and your note of broken maps to why.

To say your name is to bring you home in a wooden birdhouse.
Each time I see our Mother blow you out in Rothmans
she remembers your incense, the birth and still deaths.

To say your name is to admit you go to God grey and cold.
Each time I see our Father he is a cradle of bone.
There are holes instead of eyes – tomb dark.

Unearthing you is the colour of Facebook blues and reds.
Ninety-four comments that say nothing and everything.
Sixty-three emoticons weep at a coffin of pixels.

The Gonorrhea Soldiers

Dubbed "penis propaganda," these attractive women were deliberately drawn with deeply etched red lips designed to entice a man into paying attention to something that wasn't talked about openly: sexually transmitted diseases."

– CNN

Eugene left Hilda roses and the clap,
with a killer line borrowed from Olivier –
passed off as his own in her husband's gown.
How she swooned into Sunday until Tuesday.

Eugene made many things: wheat in Utah,
and bastards in Manchester bedrooms,
who lined the dance floors of *Our blessed Mary.*
Sold by a bartering Nun by an Aryan Jesus.

Eugene blew Lucky Strike halos to Angels,
made devils of them pinned like vinyl to music,
handing them a folded hanky with 'E' to remember him.
They never forgot him when the penny dropped.

Eugene left his wife wheat and instructions.
She carried them out to the letter.
"How handsome my Eugene was," she told the pastor,
"how rotten the wheat is this year."

Part VII:
Nine Eleven & the Hidden Massacres

"Humankind has not woven the web of life. We are but one thread within it. Whatever we do to the web, we do to ourselves. All; things are bound together. All things connect."

– Chief Seattle, Suquamish & Duwamish Native American tribes.

The Falling Man

On nine twelve they spoke of the falling man.
Imagine developing his shape from water,
it gradually appearing in bleak suspension.
Leave him to dry into more than shapes.
Watch black grains form into her son.
I heard the sky was perfect blue.
On nine-thirteen you said they resembled rain.
Maybe some were whole new worlds.
White cotton should not turn scarlet,
it should not lay by twisted steel.
A mother is nationless in birth.
Her children belong to life.
I heard he was born
imperfectly human.
They erased him.

Flight 93

"He wanted me to recite the Lord's Prayer with him. And he did. He recited the Lord's Prayer from start to finish"
– Mrs Jefferson, regarding passenger Todd Beamer.

In our first moments we arrive in motherships.
They sever the belt she had fastened around us
and we are hijacked into earth weeping for peace.
I like to think we leave in the same way, *but no.*

In final moments we become otherworldly.
We recite the Lord's Prayer with a stranger.
Words become safeguarded sacraments.
"Tell my wife I love her. *She'll know,* but tell her"

In final moments a spork can be a wooden spear.
A lowly office worker can be a gladiator, a shield.
When black clouds billow into our blue-sky town *we'll know.*
Let them see corn cover our tomb, no names please.

Last night I took a moment to think of old America.
My mind filled with smoke and I read the Lord's prayer.
I trespassed my lips on to the face of my wife and I thought,
she will forgive me for my failings as she smiles before seriousness.

Baghdad Zoo
After Elaine Christie & Leanne Bridgewater

There was a place in the municipal cosmos
where bomb craters became bird baths
and garlands of foxes slept in tyres.

At Baghdad Zoo you could hear music in a tiger's eye.
You could roam the Serengeti there
as far away as Babylon and Mars.

A sniper made an exploding rainbow.
He shot a macaw confused on the wire.
Nothing personal, just war and boredom.

At Baghdad zoo a wolf could have left its enclosure.
He thought the moon had given up on him
Jailed in ribs, the heart packs up like a market watch.

It is easy to herd kept animals back to where they belong,
they are nothing but eyes floating like dead planets.
Here in the cosmos of Iraq it is the end of worlds.

The Bear of Sarajevo Zoo

I picture her starving,
mouth pinked by eating her inmates.
From a distance her jaw resembled a carnation floating.

A leaf with a bullet-hole spirals into the painted forest.
This is her last meal and the zookeeper roars
The bear is quiet. Sarajevo is quieter now.

Three years ago she gave birth in a plastic moulded cave.
The bonfire of her birthing blew smoke into the cold.
Blood-warm against her teats they were safe.

I picture her running.
Exposed on a plateau split by streams silvered by salmon.
They have come home exhausted, to lay eggs, to fatten her.

Three Landay Poems for an Afghan Sunrise

Child, you shall see my face uncovered,
like sun through sky and dandelions through black asphalt.

Husband, you shall feel my heart on yours,
pulsing with heatwaves we will kiss watchful eyes of sky.

After the prying mountains and starlit drones
peace comes in the returning birds to returning rain.

To Pull the Head From a Flower
After Ken Bigley & Daniel Pearl

He told his wife
the field will burn yellow with yarrow in winter,
but first they must dead head the flowers.

He told his friend
to pinch the necks gently as if she was patting
the hill where their son sleeps till January.

He told his lover
when you pull a root from a dying flower
a blackbird caws from the blossom then dies.

He told his Sarah,
to pat the soil how their hearts felt at Heathrow.
She fed the earth then buried the heads.

They told his widow
he wasn't afraid, kneeling in the sand,
her long black flower of shadows.

Srebrenica Massacre
For the 8000 Muslims massacred in 1994

I had to work harder to learn about you.
It's as if you were killed twice-over:
first by gun, then by side column.
If only you were fashionable,
then I could find you,
share you, like you,
add emoticons.
Srebrenica.

To find the doves we must look for crows:
the smiling architect shaking hands;
peacekeepers overrun by minions.
Imagine Father and son lined up,
Twin towers over the ground,
two bullets smashing skulls.
Bone matter, *don't matter.*
Page nine of a paper,
known for a day.
If only you were
fashionable.

War Bird

What was that ragged meat the magpie brought?
Clouds should not emerge from Belgian mud.
Man has made himself cloud and rudiment.

Why are bloody mouthed dogs barking at sky?
Wolves should not reply to their brethren.
The wolf eye woods are a star-belt.

How did the budgerigar escape into the Oak?
A sparrow-hawk sensed it was tamed,
pinned down its wing and a song died.

A Woman Soldier Opens Fire

"Syrian children wanted to divert Pokemaniac's attention to their plight, they hold placards with Pokemon on it, asks Pokemon Go fans to catch them."

– India Today

Her skin was Pikachu yellow,
nobody looked for the monster in her.
The florist's daughter, retching from her ointment,
cared not if the fire was Russian or Brexit-European.
Flames hurt, wherever they are forged and baptised from.

The furious doctor has not slept for eleven Iraqi nights.
He is shaking so violently, *yet gently* injects Shoab. And
tonight, in penicillin dreams, Shoab may walk again. Walk
to his Mother and see a red scarf leave her mouth
and strike her down where she tucked him in.

It is time to look for Pokémon in wartime.
For three seconds the woman soldier opens fire.
She is a woman soldier and last night was a mere child.
For three minutes her Father was a florist of wounds and cyclamen
laid it on her grave, *her womanly bones.*
All they found was a monster.

Instructions on a Successful Remembrance

This is your first remembrance.
Poppies begin life as black seeds
and primary colours come secondly:
pink for the flesh of man,
red for the blood of pawn,
orange for the final dusk,
white for eyes turned back in their sockets,
yellow for the gangrenous wound.
purple for the war horse running in sleep.

This is your second remembrance.
Poppies can be pinned down by wind.
Not a single soul but a wren could see
how flowers dance in the ivory soil,
how poppies were first worn by farm-hand lovers.

This is your last remembrance.
Wear the wind and picture the fallen.
Watch crows chase buzzards from blotted trees.
Hear the world in two minutes not observing silence,
remember that poppies do not grow through lapels or Haig.
They start black and do not choose the creed or colour of opiate.
Smell the ground sweet with life, not serpentine in spilled intestines.

Red for the cheeks of Conor who ran to sign on.
White for the protruding bone of Khan now gone.
Orange for the star that pulls our tides and flowers.
Purple for the squaddie who hears an engine backfire and cowers.
Pink for the embryo inside a widow who considers abortion.
Yellow for her jaundiced daughter who grew from water.
Love for the mother who writhes like poppies in torsion.

Imagining Wilfred Owen's 104th Birthday

After Neil Young

If you lived to see the maddened lions
would you say a few words to camera four,
And shake the hand of a corporate sponsor,
then read half of a poem before cutting to a break?

I'd love to see your mother's milk in your cataracts
well up where no man should stay in the eternal eye.
I'd love to hear you use the old term "shell-shock"
and Kay Burley from Sky apologise to the viewers for it.

If you lived to meet Keith from Rochdale back from Basra,
would you recognise that Keith from Rochdale is missing?
Would you let him say the C-word without shunning him?
Could Keith find his way home through deep red valleys on his wrists?

I'd love to see Boris Johnson take a selfie of you both by the lions,
and you'd say to him "Did you get shot at dawn dancing on my grave?
I'd love to see you drunk in a wheelchair being pushed by Keith,
and the red of Keith's poppy, and the red of his piss bag on wire.

I'd love to see you alive in the encore of your 'Anthem for Doomed Youth'.

A Syrian Slam Poet Dies with Her Mouth Open

Just weeks ago
a Syrian slam poet screamed stanzas under her breath.
She knows how Kalashnikovs sound,
like her Father rat-a-tatting her door
that night when she French-kissed a forbidden boy.

A Syrian poet lived with her mouth open
that first time she read aloud Rumi.
Her breath dissolved bluing a window.
She touched herself into a woman *to let the girl go.*

Just seconds ago
she performed her poem to the tomahawk sky.
These are not real tomahawks, for they would scalp the top of the world.
Remove the brain and see that its swirls are the very fingerprints of God herself.

She screamed to the sky: *"I am woman, a goddess of the shooting star.*
The trebuchet light that swirls into sycamore to be one with earth."
To be" …

Transmission ends

Notes

The Projectionist's Lullaby

Due to thousands of facial disfigurements inflicted upon soldiers some park benches in Sidcup, England, were painted blue, a warning to citizens that anyone sitting on these benches would be distressing to look at.

– Smithsonian

The Munitionettes FC

"The Government encouraged women to play football as the games boosted morale and reinforced the image that women were capable of jobs deemed only appropriate for men. All of the matches women played in also raised money for War charities."

– The Collection

Senryu for Guernica

Guernica is largely considered the first city targeted for civilian bombings.

Dogfight Over Sandwich Bay

During the Battle of Britain 544 pilots lost their lives. A further 795 would die before the end of World War II.

– Battle of Britain London Monument

Hundreds of pilots who migrated to serve in the Battle of Britain were from Czechoslovakia, Poland, Canada, Australasia, Ireland, Canada, the Caribbean, and the USA.

Merlin, a liquid cooled V-12 engine produced by Rolls Royce and fitted in the Hurricane.

Sikh Soldier

3.8 million British Indian soldiers served in World War I & II alongside many others enlisted from the British Empire. Thousands of these soldiers were also Muslims – Gakkar, Awan, Pashtunwani, Jag, Mughal – including warrior races of the Punjab.

– BBC, British Army Museum, The Spectator, The Independent and J. Mahmood.

Lidice

On June 10, 1942 the German government announced that it had destroyed the small village of Lidice, Czechoslovakia, killing 340 citizens. Surviving women and children were then deported to concentration camps; or, if found suitable to be 'Germanized', sent to the Greater Reich. The Nazis then proclaimed that the village of Lidice and its residents were now erased from memory.

– Lidice Memorial & Holocaust / Education and Research Project / Smithsonian.

Stalingrad

According to the World War II Museum, New Orleans, it is reported that Russia lost twenty-four million soldiers and civilians compared to under 420,000 Americans (Approximately 50 times more than America)

P.O.W.

During World War II the Japanese Armed Forces captured nearly 140,000 Allied military personnel (Australia, Canada, Great Britain, India, Netherlands, New Zealand, and the United States) in Southeast Asia and the Pacific areas. They were forced to engage in the hard labour of constructing railways, roads, airfields, etc. to be used by the Japanese Armed Forces in the occupied areas.

– Forces War Records

Pearl

Statistics for Pearl Harbour: "in total, 2,403 Americans were killed during the attack. 68 were civilians."

– pearlharbor.org

Zeke, or the Mitsubishi A6M, was the primary offensive aircraft used by the Japanese military in World War II.

Enola Gay

"If I had the choice. I'd wipe 'em out. You're gonna kill innocent people at the same time, but we've never fought a damn war anywhere in the world where they didn't kill innocent people. If the newspapers would just cut out the shit: "You've killed so many civilians." That's their tough luck for being there."

– Paul Tibbetts, Pilot of the Enola Gay (interviewed by The Guardian in 2002)

Enola Gay was the name of the plane that dropped the atomic bomb over Hiroshima killing and injuring approximately 140,000 people. It was named after pilot, Paul Tibbetts', mother.

The Suicide of Private John Doe

In 2012 more British soldiers died from suicide than those killed in conflict.

– Stripes, The Telegraph, BBC etc.

For Syrian Boys Who Will Never Kiss a Woman

"An unprecedented 65.6 million people around the world have been forced from home by conflict and persecution at the end of 2016. Among them are nearly 22.5 million refugees, over half of whom are under the age of 18."

– United Nations

Dead Babes Stolen for Nuclear Tests

"Media reports have said 6,000 dead babies were snatched from hospitals in Australia, Britain, Canada, Hong Kong, the United States and South America for over 15 years without parental consent, and shipped to America for atomic tests."

–CNN – June 2001

Letters of Last Resort

According to the 2008 nuclear war documentary The Human Button (featured on BBC Radio 4), there were four known options given to the Prime Minister to include in the letters of last resort. The Prime Minister instructs the submarine commander to: 1) retaliation 2) non-retaliation 3) using own judgement 4) place submarine under the command of another Allied country such as Australia or USA.

Maralinga

As with previous British nuclear weapons tests at Emu Field, the local Aboriginal population bore the brunt of radiation exposure.

– Nuclear Risks

Revelations in a recent book, *Maralinga,* by Frank Walker showed how British scientists secretly used the affected Australian population to study the long-term effects of radiation exposure, much like the Americans did with Marshall Islanders. Although the scientists involved began by testing animal bones, they soon moved on to humans. A directive was issued by UK scientists to "Bring me the bones of Australian babies, the more the better," an experimentation that lasted 21 years.

– Beyond Nuclear International

What Churchill Said by the Feet of Jesus Christ and Gary Oldman

"I hate Indians," he (Churchill) told the Secretary of State for India, Leopold Amery. "They are a beastly people with a beastly religion." The famine was their own fault, he declared at a war-cabinet meeting, for "breeding like rabbits."

The Bengali famine in India during World War II is estimated to have killed over 3-4 million people. 2.5 million Indians fought for the British Empire in WWII.

– various

The Bear of Sarajevo Zoo

After surviving the siege of Sarajevo for more than 200 days, a bear, the last surviving animal in the zoo here, has died.

– *New York Times*, November 1992

Acknowledgments

We would like to thank the editors of the following publications where these poems first appeared:

Envoi, The Journal of The Wilfred Owen Association, Warscapes, Under the Radar, Peace Insight, Eyewear in the *Refugees Welcome Anthology, Lacuna Magazine* (Warwick University Human Rights), *National Army Poetry Competition 2018 Prize-winners' Anthology, The Wilfred Owen Story, Verve Poetry Anthology Eighty Four: Poems on Male Suicide*, Ekstasis Press & Asylum Magazine in the *Voicing Suicide Anthology, Ink Sweat & Tears, International Times, The Twin Project, Snakeskin, Picaroon, Now Then Magazine, Amaryllis, Until the Stars Burn Out, Riggwelter Journal, Proletarian Poetry, Dark River Literary Journal, Penance, I Am Not a Silent Poet, Fresh Air Magazine, The Curly Mind, The Broken Bugle, Interrogative Papers, Wren & Rook Journal,* the *Voices 1919 Anthology,* & *Dreamcatcher*.

Other notable publications & features:

National Army Poetry Competition 2018: Writing Armistice. Winner of the Museum of Military Medicine Category for 'A Black Nurse Tends to Wounds'.

Several poems in this colection were translated into Arabic for a research journal by the Humanities Department of King Saud University.

Lidice was an *Ink Sweat & Tears* pick of the month finalist for September 2018.

'The Bear of Sarajevo Zoo' was commissioned by The Coventry Project of Biennial Art as part of The Twin Project, which connected themes of peace between international cities twinned with Coventry.

'Enola Gay' is a donated peace education resource for Quakers Peace Education UK and CND Peace Education UK and was included in a Quakers UK Peace Podcast discussion about modern conflict and Peace Education resources in January 2018.

'Rambo of Kinshasa' was nominated as Best of the net at Dark Water Literary Journal in 2016

'A Black Nurse Tends to Wounds' was read and recorded in the ruins of Coventry Cathedral for Armistice on 11/11/2018.

'P.O.W.' was first published in *The Dreaded Boy* by Pighog Press.

Several Hiroshima and Nagasaki poems have been taught by Professor R Klein at poetry workshop classes in Hiroshima and performed for CND, Coventry Cathedral and Positive Images Festival.

Thanks to Andrea Mbarushimana for the book cover image *Intrusion*© and *Aftermath*©.

Thanks also to Coventry Cathedral Plumbline Arts Festival, Salisbury International Arts Festival, Coventry Positive Images Festival, BBC CWR, Hillz FM, Coventry Peace Festival, Leamington Peace Festival where many of these poems were also performed.

Finally love and thanks to my wife Joanne and my writing sentinel Joseph for keeping the halo of light visible on this long cold descent into the darkness to find the fragments of hope from conflict. Thanks to Matthew Geden for his support and insight and finally to Alec Newman at Knives, Forks and Spoons Press for providing a space for these poems to live.

Images:

p.3, *Aftermath,* by Andrea Mbarushimana.

p.9, Photo by C. Sutch.

p.21, *Belchite*, by Pedrosala.

p.49, *Volgograd*, by Aleksey.

p.61, *Car of the doctor in Oradour sur Glane*, by Ivonne Wierink.

p.73, *Part of the Hiroshima Peace Memorial in Hiroshima, Japan*, by Purplebear.

p.81, *The Separation or Security Wall Between Gaza and Israel*, by Michiel.

p.95, *City of Aleppo in Aerial View, Filmed by a Drone, Syria*, by Smallcreative.

Lightning Source UK Ltd.
Milton Keynes UK
UKHW020833240919
350291UK00001B/8/P